YOUR KNOWLEDGE HAS VALUE

Stanko Radmilovic

When and how the ideas of classical liberalism mutated into a modern, repressive market fundamentalism

Inflation and economic growth in the light of public spending, monetary aggregates and unemployment. Comparative analysis: 69 countries, 2000-12

GRIN Verlag

Bibliografische Information der Deutschen Nationalbibliothek:

Die Deutsche Bibliothek verzeichnet diese Publikation in der Deutschen National-bibliografie; detaillierte bibliografische Daten sind im Internet über http://dnb.d-nb.de/ abrufbar.

Imprint:

Copyright © 2013 GRIN Verlag GmbH
Druck und Bindung: Books on Demand GmbH, Norderstedt Germany
ISBN: 978-3-656-59135-1

GRIN - Your knowledge has value

Der GRIN Verlag publiziert seit 1998 wissenschaftliche Arbeiten von Studenten, Hochschullehrern und anderen Akademikern als eBook und gedrucktes Buch. Die Verlagswebsite www.grin.com ist die ideale Plattform zur Veröffentlichung von Hausarbeiten, Abschlussarbeiten, wissenschaftlichen Aufsätzen, Dissertationen und Fachbüchern.

Visit us on the internet:

http://www.grin.com/

http://www.facebook.com/grincom

http://www.twitter.com/grin_com

Prof. dr Stanko Radmilovic

When and how the ideas of classical liberalism mutated into a modern, repressive the market fundamentalism

Inflation, economic growth, in the light of public spending, monetary aggregates and unemployment - Comparative factography with brief preliminary potentiation - 69 countries, 2000-12

We could say that the lower factography are specifically aimed to the performance analysis of the neoliberal doctrine of market fundamentalism: research the economic performance of those countries that the strictly applied, those who are forced to do so and those that implement various heterodox modality.

It will be useful, even necessary to present the to readers a few quotes / views from the emphasis on the what's in them have an impact on the determination to formulate preliminarnie reviews and makes suggestions more complete, deeper analysis.

Let us start with a quote that, I believe, best expresses the idea, the root from which sprang the doctrine of market fundamentalism in the applied sense. Quote dates from a later period of time when Hayek and others affirmed the concept and theory of economic liberalism embodied in the famous phrase Laissez faire et laissez passer..

Perhaps to the surprise of many, I have in mind a much less "overhyped" views of Milton Friedman. Why the Surprise? Well, because he is better known as the creator of monetarism, "Chicago School" monetarist counter-revolution against the "Keynesian revolution". In fact, strengthens the idea that Kenes views about money has implicaton Which are proinflation.

But here I think of a much broader and far-reaching issues that can be seen from the following quote (emphasis is mine):

> *"Different types of structural disorder and inelasticities may come into play and prevent the achievement of the long-term hypothetical position of equilibrium under conditions of full employment; dynamic changes in technology, resources, and social and economic institutions can continually change the characteristics of the equilibrium position, however, there is any fundamental 'deficiency in price system' that caused unemployment to be a natural consequence of an efficient market mechanism. This (Keynes, ed. RS) setting has played a significant role in recruiting many economists to Keynesianism, particularly the large number of reformers, social critics and radicals were convinced that there is something fundamentally wrong in the capitalist 'system' ..."*

Milton Friedman, Teorija novca i monetarna politika, prevod, Beograd, 1973, str. 161. i 162.

The same opinion on Friedman's impact on the market-fundamentalist views expressed and Nobel laureate Stiglitz. He says *"that Friedman and his followers contributed to the causes of the current turmoil,"* The Chicago School bears the responsibility for intellectual grounding a notion that markets are capable to self-regulation"*, which we presented in a short article on this site Kraj dominacije monetarizma?

These are, no doubt, the premise on which the aforementioned market fundamentalism. It goes without saying that the above premises on to price mechanism - the market system without fundamental shortcomings had to be the best in most developed countries. And this would be the country in terms of inflation, economic growth and unemployment, they had to show the best performance. And if that is the case, then it would have to be clearly visible (from factography in the table below) that accrues to non-market disturbances coming from the fiscal and monetary areas.

And vice versa, should be visible in the other, emerging market countries with weaker, uncompletely developed market mechanism (system). They should, therefore, had to exert poorer performance - lower growth and higher inflation (in column 4 indices abowe 100) and a higher unemployment rate. Particularly if, in addition, is coming and larger disturbances in the area of public spending and in monetary area.

At this point, we have, for now, just to satisfy the observation that the empirical data in the table below, the premise of this market fundamentalism more deny than confirm. Still more complex and deeper analysis (both mine and others who feel able to do so) in the table contained and other empirical data, should it in an argumentative way refute or to prove that they are correct.

Inflation, economic growth, their correlation, in the light of public (government) spending, the growth of monetary aggregates and the unemployment rate

Data sources and authentic categorical explanations are below the table

Country	GDP percentages of constant price, year-on-year changes percent change; averages 2000-12	Inflation: Annual percentages of average consumer prices are year-on-year changes; averages 2000-12	Indices of instability: rates of inflation (col. 3) / rates of growth (col. 2) / * 100	Real (deflated) the growth of general government total expenditure (annual in %); averages 2000-12	Money and quasi money growth (annual %)	Unemployment rate (% of total labor force); averages 2000-12
1	2	3	4	5	6	7
Albania	5,1	2,8	54,9	3,6	11,0	1,4
Angola	10,1	64,7	640,6	8,7	18,3	...
Argentina	4,3	8,9	207,0	8,9	82,3	12,2
Australia	3,1	3,0	96,8	3,6	10,2	5,4
Austria	1,7	2,0	117,6	1,5	35,1	4,4
Azerbaijan	11,9	6,7	56,3	19,2	5,6	6,9
Belarus	6,7	37,9	565,7	33,2	61,5	25,2
Belgium	1,5	2,3	153,3	2,3	4,2	7,7
B - H	3,2	2,8	87,5	1,5	16,6	29,0
Brazil	3,4	6,6	194,1	4,5	17,0	9,0
Bulgaria	3,8	5,9	155,3	2,9	17,9	11,7
Canada	2,2	2,1	95,5	2,0	16,6	7,1
Chile	4,4	3,3	75,0	4,6	8,6	8,7
China	10,0	2,3	23,0	13,7	17,5	4,0
Croatia	2,1	3,0	142,9	0,8	13,3	12,8
Cyprus	2,4	2,7	112,5	3,9	10,0	5,5
Czech R.	3,0	2,7	90,0	3,7	7,2	7,1
Denmark	0,8	2,2	275,0	1,2	6,1	5,3

Estonia	4,8	4,3	89,6	6,5	20,6	10,2
Finland	2,0	2,0	100,0	2,7	7,6	8,3
France	1,3	1,8	138,5	1,8	6,6	9,1
Germany	1,3	1,7	130,8	1,1	2,4	8,4
Greece	0,8	3,2	400,0	1,3	3,0	11,6
Hungary	1,9	5,8	305,3	1,7	9,6	7,9
India	7,0	6,6	94,3	8,2	16,8	...
Indonesia	5,3	7,7	145,3	7,3	13,5	8,4
Iran	4,6	16,3	354,3	5,2	15,2	12,5
Ireland	3,1	2,4	77,4	6,0	9,1	7,4
Israel	3,8	2,1	55,3	2,0	6,0	10,1
Italy	0,4	2,4	600,0	1,0	8,3	8,2
Japan	0,9	-0,3	-33,3	1,7	-0,3	4,7
Kazakhstan	8,1	8,7	107,4	9,1	33,9	7,9
Korea	4,3	3,1	72,1	5,6	15,6	3,6
Latvia	4,4	4,9	111,4	4,3	16,5	12,1
Lithuania	4,6	3,0	65,2	4,8	15,2	11,9
Macedonia	2,6	2,9	111,5	2,3	17,7	33,6
Mexico	2,3	4,9	213,0	4,3	9,4	3,9
Moldova	4,6	10,7	232,6	6,4	26,3	6,8
Montenegro	3,1	13,7	441,9	5,6	33,6	...
Netherlands	1,4	2,2	157,1	2,2	8,2	4,0
New Zeal.	2,5	2,6	104,0	3,0	6,7	5,2
Nigeria	8,4	12,3	146,4	7,7	27,5	15,3
Norway	1,7	1,9	111,8	2,1	7,9	3,6
Pakistan	4,5	8,2	182,2	6,0	15,0	6,8
Peru	5,6	2,7	48,2	5,6	10,0	8,5
Philippines	4,8	4,7	97,9	3,8	9,6	9,2
Poland	3,8	3,5	92,1	4,3	10,0	13,8
Portugal	0,5	2,6	520,0	1,1	7,2	8,1
Qatar	12,5	4,5	36,0	14,7	23,5	...
Romania	3,7	13,8	373,0	4,0	22,0	7,1
Russia	5,2	12,3	236,5	5,8	31,3	7,7
S. Arabia	5,4	2,1	38,9	5,7	12,9	1,0
Serbia	3,2	19,4	606,3	6,8	42,5	18,2
Slovak R.	4,2	4,7	111,9	4,9	8,9	18,2
Slovenia	2,3	4,3	187,0	2,9	...	6,5
So. Africa	3,5	5,9	168,6	5,5	13,6	25,0
Spain	1,9	2,9	152,6	3,1	10,8	13,9
Sweden	2,4	1,5	62,5	1,8	10,8	6,7
Switzerland	1,8	0,8	44,4	1,3	4,6	2,8
Thailand	4,2	2,7	64,3	6,6	8,2	1,2

Tunisia	3,9	3,5	89,7	5,6	10,6	14,1
Turkey	4,5	19,7	437,8	3,3	26,8	10,2
Ukraine	4,4	11,5	261,4	6,9	32,7	8,4
UA Emirat.	5,8	4,5	77,6	6,2	17,6	...
UK	1,8	2,2	122,2	3,7	8,2	6,0
US	1,8	2,5	138,9	3,2	6,2	6,3
Uzbekistan	6,9	15,0	217,4	6,2	...	0,3
Venezuela	3,7	21,9	591,9	8,5	39,3	11,3
Vietnam	6,9	8,0	115,9	9,9	28,2	5,2

Source of data: IMF World Economic Outlook Database, April 2013 and for coll. 6 WB Databank, 18. september 2013

Authentic categorical explanations:

In coli.2 - GDP percentages of constant price, year-on-year changes percent change; Annual percentages of constant price GDP are year-on-year changes; the base year is country-specific . Expenditure-based GDP is total final expenditures at purchasers' prices (including the f.o.b. value of exports of goods and services), less the f.o.b. value of imports of goods and services. [SNA 1993]

In coll. 3 - Inflation: Annual percentages of average consumer prices are year-on-year changes; Annual percentages of average consumer prices are year-on-year changes.

In coll. 5 - Real (deflated) the growth of general government total expenditure (annual in %); Total expenditure consists of total expense and the net acquisition of nonfinancial assets. Note: Apart from being on an accrual basis, total expenditure differs from the GFSM 1986 definition of total expenditure in the sense that it also takes the disposals of nonfinancial assets into account. The GDP deflator is derived by dividing current price GDP by constant price GDP and is considered to be an alternate measure of inflation. Data are expressed in the base year of each country's national accounts.

In coll. 6 - Money and quasi money growth (annual %): Average annual growth rate in money and quasi money. Money and quasi money comprise the sum of currency outside banks, demand deposits other than those of the central government, and the time, savings, and foreign currency deposits of resident sectors other than the central government. This definition is frequently called M2; it corresponds to lines 34 and 35 in the International Monetary Fund's (IMF) International Financial Statistics (IFS). The change in the money supply is measured as the difference in end-of-year totals relative to the level of M2 in the preceding year.

In col. 7 - Unemployment rate (Percent of total labor force); Unemployment rate can be defined by either the national definition, the ILO harmonized definition, or the OECD harmonized definition. The OECD harmonized unemployment rate gives the number of unemployed persons as a percentage of the labor force (the total number of people employed plus unemployed). [OECD Main Economic Indicators, OECD, monthly] As defined by the International Labour Organization, unemployed workers are those who are currently not working but are willing and able to work for pay, currently available to work, and have actively searched for work. [ILO, http://www.ilo.org/public/english/bureau/stat/res/index.htm]